Just a Tumble Down the Hill

Alicia Martinez

BookLeaf
Publishing

India | USA | UK

Just a Tumble Down the Hill © 2024 Alicia
Martinez

All rights reserved.

No part of this publication may be
reproduced, stored in a retrieval system, or
transmitted, in any form or by any means,
electronic, mechanical, photocopying,
recording or otherwise, without the prior
written permission of the presenters.

Alicia Martinez asserts the moral right to be
identified as the author of this work.

Presentation by *BookLeaf Publishing*

Web: www.bookleafpub.com

E-mail: info@bookleafpub.com

ISBN: 9789363301245

First edition 2024

ACKNOWLEDGEMENT

I have to give all of my thanks to the following:

My mom and stepdad, who gave encouragement and celebrated when I told them I was doing this.

To the best friends in the world, Mary and Brittany, who helped me through my anxiety of writing this book and gave me constructive criticism.

To my old English teacher Mr. Daiss, who read every single poem, helped with edits, and made suggestions to make this book readable.

And finally, the relationships and events that taught me new aspects of myself and inspired many of these poems.

PREFACE

These twenty-one poems are filled with my thoughts when life honestly sucked. They deal with grief, miscarriages, the end of a relationship, feeling completely desolate, and trying to handle anxiety. They are not all sad though, there will be poems scattered with hope, lessons learned, and strength gained.

The title was inspired by a recent event in which I actually fell down a hill during a hike. I ended up getting lost, got a concussion, and somehow managed to find the trail again. Seemed to fit the journey of my life as I still enjoyed the hike and went back a day later.

Overall, I hope if you find a poem that resonates with you, whether it's one of hope or loss you know you are not alone and we are all just tumbling down a hill trying to make the most of it.

The Prayer in the Rain

To smile
and have it stay on my face
To dance
and have no fear
To love
and have it towards myself
To hope
and not give up in the storms
To dream
and make them all happen

I Remember You

I remember your arms around me
Your smile that made a bad day good

I remember your laugh as if you were beside me
And your eyes that sparkled in the sun

I remember your heart
The beat of it lulled me to sleep

I remember you

Your lips, hands, the way you walked and loved

I miss you

I miss you with every breath
I miss you through life and death

I miss you
And I'm sorry I left you

The Dance

Two flowers danced
Vibrant and full of life
One was older and the other younger

They would dance
When the sun rose
And when it fell
Carefree and unaware
Of the darkness that was watching

Then it happened
With a butterfly passing
The young flower was taken away

Yet, the old flower
Continued to dance
Hoping for her flower again

She danced when the sun rose
She danced when it fell
She danced even as the ground went pale

She continued to dance
As she began to wilt
As her petals

Slowly fell

She continued to dance
Even as she became bare
through the wear and tear
Hoping, for her flower again

Then a wind came so cold and quick
Almost blowing the old flower away
As the wind faded two months later that day
There was another young flower to fill the rift

They began to dance
As the old flower felt renewed
They began to dance
As her petals grew

They danced
No longer feeling cold or their wounds
They danced as the sun rose
And danced as it fell

And when the darkness came
And took the young flower again

The old flower continued to dance

She danced when the sun rose
She danced when it fell

She danced even as the ground went pale

She continued to dance
As she began to wilt
As her petals
Began to slowly fall

She continued to dance
Though her wounds laid bare

She continued to dance
Through the wear and tear

She danced for the daughters who fell

My Grief

A hole pulsating
Commanding attention
The edges never healing
They are always trembling

Encapsulating every breath
Leaving aches in my chest

The hole is never-ending
Just a void-taking
What was once bright and full of light
Has turned dull, gray, and stuck in the night

Sometimes it's small
Easy to put behind
Some days it's large
And consumes my mind

I can't fill the hole
The one in my chest

I can't ignore
The aches and pain

It all needs to be felt

Demands it be so

I feel and deal
With all that comes
I don't know what else to do

Forgive

A word filled with so much regret and hope
Regret for things said and actions done
Hope to move on and obtain a future

It can be easily done
Or take years to give

A word I'm *intimately* familiar with

Forgive
All those who hurt me?
Done.

Forgive myself?

I can't.

I can't forgive myself
For all the hurt I caused
For the lives I lost
For when my mind and body failed

Forgive

I forgive those who hurt me

I give them the peace and hope they desire
I give it freely for their lives and mine

But forgive myself?

The anger I feel towards myself
For failing to improve
Failing to be the good Daughter
Sister
Wife
And Partner

Failing to keep those two lives safe

Forgive

Forgive

Forgive myself

I Have Sad Days

When everything is bright and cheerful
but feels muted and wrong
When everything is right
but I feel gone

It could be the happiest of days
Cheerful music playing
but all I hear is a sorrowful melody

I have sad days
When I don't want them
I want to be happy
but they refuse to leave

I'm having a sad day
but I can't tell you what's wrong

There's good in my life
but I'm still forlorn

I want to be happy
but it's a sad day

And I feel alone

Baffled

I try
I really am trying

To make this work
I've put in so much effort and time

But still
It doesn't feel enough

I don't know what to do
I'm trying but not succeeding

WTF

Why did I think it was okay?

I found the countless writings
Of all the ways I failed

Wasn't doing enough
"Doing too much"
And all the things to make it okay

Countless deadlines

three months to get it together

six months or we are done

One more year

and you are "done"

Why the fuck

did I stay?

I Want

I want to remember the joy
The feeling of new beginnings
That sparkle of life in my chest

I want to feel the sun again
The warmth on my skin

I want to smile
And for it to be real

I want the happiness
And to be me again

I want the confidence
And the joy of being free

I want all of this and more
And I will obtain it

Confidence

I love the woman I see—

With the lines on her forehead--
And the ones around her mouth
And the crow's feet by her eyes

I can trace the constellations on her body
By the freckles adorning her face and thighs

I can see the joy of the pudge on her belly
And the "dips" in her hips

I love the stories that her body tells

The scars on her knees
The ones that mark her elbows
Even the scores on her wrist

I see in the mirror a woman I love

New Laugh

I found a new laugh today

It was ironic
Full of disbelief and spite

A short
"HA!"
That rises in pitch as it ends

A laugh born from a heart broken
From life's one too many "kicks"

I don't like this new laugh

The One Who Stands

A man stands
His shoulders burdened
And with a heavy heart

Scars littered across his body and soul
Yet, he hides them behind an impenetrable wall

His hands carry them when they are weak
His mind gives them the wisdom they seek
His mouth gives reassurance to the meek

He bears the weight of people
Never a "thank you" received

He is the laughter, the Jester
The Friend, the Lover
He will be whatever they need

But I ask, what about him?

Who reaches out to this man with weary eyes?
Who carries him when he is weak?
Who dries the tears that fall on his cheek?

Why do those who call him a friend

Watch and let him stumble and fall
Over and over again?

If they could only see
The pain inside that he keeps
That beyond the grin there is
A man who weeps

The Unattainable

There I look
But never far
That I see
I long to be.

I search
But don't find
I long
As it passes by.

I wander
I seek
A light
A feeling—

Just something

A place beyond my heart.

Happiness

I'm finding new things
Joys I didn't know
Strengths I possess
And soft things to caress

I'm learning to shine
Get freedom from doubt
Find love in myself
And leave nothing to rest

I'm enjoying life
In all of the paths
The straight and narrow
And the ones that curve

There Was Good

There were laughs
Comforts on really bad days

Getting groceries was actually fun

I learned about so many new games
And I had fun even when I didn't win

There was so much love
And so much joy

(There was six years)

And there was good

The Man Next to Me

His face looks troubled,
Silent and hard.
His thoughts wander,
To the forbidden parts of his mind.

He glances around with his eyes

I wonder what he is thinking
With those mysterious eyes
I wonder what he hides.

That Which Remains

Who am I after we end?
What do I like,
And what will I watch again?
Is my laughter the same
Or has that also changed?

I'm struggling to define
Where you end and I begin.

Was I actually me
Or someone playing pretend?

I didn't realize how much I lost
How much I changed for you

So here I am.

Trying to figure out:
What parts are *me*?
What parts are *you*?

The Sprite

I remember the girl who twirled
Who laughed as she fell

I remember the girl who would smile
All teeth for you to see

She was innocent and wild
Scraped knees
And stung by bees

Yes, I remember that foolish child.

She had worries and fears
But still pursued life

I remember her endless curiosity
Finding her in nooks and crannies

Yes, I remember that wild child.

She wore her heart on her sleeve
Shined bright for herself
She sang and hummed her melodies
Full of joy and life

I remember the girl I used to be.

She lives on in my memories
But I hope to one day set her free.

A Breath

So simple
But profound
All the worries,
The stress,
Being released
In just a breath
I feel peace
A knowing
Of my path
I feel at home
In that breath

Fall Slowly

I jump in too fast
Ruled by my emotions

I want to ravish you
And be loved by you

Yet, I remind myself
To slow down and stop

For once, I don't want to jump

Rather I want to fall
Enjoy every experience

I want to wade the waters
Enjoy every stroke
Touch
Look
Conversation

I want to fall slowly

So I ignore the urge to jump
And let my emotions stay humbled

I'm Okay

It's difficult
And tiring
I sometimes doubt my choice

Yet

I've laughed more today than in the past six
years
I have gray in my hair that I don't hide
I've challenged myself
and put my fears aside.

I sang at the top of my lungs
and had people join me
I danced with strangers
and never felt so free.

I traveled to new locations
and fell–once or twice
I gained weight from the food I made
(and yes it was more than rice).

I sometimes cry and get scared
but I haven't run away
I created memories that I cherish

ones that get me through the day

Yes

I can safely say
That despite all the bad days

I'm okay.